Keep Your Computer Alive
And Your Sanity Intact

by Daniel A. Uitti
Illustrated by Ted Hudson

www.KeepYourComputerAlive.com

Copyright © 2005 by DaSum Company, L.L.C.

All rights reserved. No part of this book shall be reproduced or transmitted in any form or by any means, electronic, mechanical, magnetic, photographic including photocopying, recording or by any information storage and retrieval system, without permission of the publisher. No patent liability is assumed with respect to the use of information contained herein. Although every precaution has been taken in the preparation of this book, the publisher and author assume no responsibility for errors or omissions. Neither is there any liability assumed for damages resulting from the use of information contained herein.

This book contains many computer tips and hints. The computer user accepts all responsibility for purchases and computer maintenance and holds the author and publisher harmless. Stories told within this book are intended to illustrate computer maintenance issues and not to degrade the reputation of any corporation or person(s) living or dead.

ISBN: 0-9708430-2-X

Published by Wash Brook Press

Cover Design by Zenographics
www.zenographics.net

Printed in the United States of America

Printed on Recycled Paper

Published July 2005

www.KeepYourComputerAlive.com

Dedication

To Sandy

Acknowledgements

To my friends Jerry Labriola, MD and Brian Jud, who foster the idea that people should write and get published through their dedicated work with the Connecticut Authors and Publishers Association.

To Ted Hudson, who captured the spirit of this book with his illustrations.

To Beth Bruno, who edited this book and, where necessary, translated computer-speak into the English language.

To my friend Cynthia Bercowetz, who took the chance to write before I did, and proved that it can be done.

To my many friends and clients, who worked through many computer problems and issues.

Contents

Introduction	1
Basic Tips for the Untrained	5
Terms Used to Describe Windows	9
Computer Confidence	15
Surge Protectors & Uninterruptible Power Supply	17
Viruses and Anti-Virus	19
SpyWare and Pop-up Ads	23
Firewalls	27
File Sharing	29
Children Use Computers	33
Avoid SPAM	35
Be Careful Opening E-mail	39
Backup Your Data	42
Backup Media	45
Save While You Work	47
Restore Your Computer	50
Write Down Passwords & Registration Numbers	52
Scandisk, Defrag & Disk Cleanup	54
What Should I Install on My Computer?	57
Software Updates	60
Hardware Updates	62
Where Do These Wires Go?	64
Keeping Your Printer in Top Shape	68
Controlling that Wild Mouse	71
Too Many Programs Running?	73
Which Internet Provider?	75
Computer Product Rating	77
Dictionary	79
Keep Your Computer Alive CHECKLIST	97
Websites in this Book	98
Future Computers	101
Index	102
Paradigms - Computer Longevity	105

Introduction

The computer is essential to everyone. We use it to organize information. We use it to communicate. We use it with the Internet to learn more about everything. It has become a vital part of our educational, financial and productive lives. Those who fail to embrace it will inevitably become dependent on those who do.

However, the increasing dependency on computers does increase our responsibility for our computer's health and ability to do its intended tasks.

This book is not a troubleshooting guide; it is a maintenance guide. It does not recommend specific products. The recommendations in this book are designed and tested for many different computers under the Microsoft Windows 98/ME/2000/XP operating systems. Most concepts here are valid for Windows 95, as well, but a Windows 95 computer is old and ready for the scrap heap. Get ready to say "goodbye" to that Windows 95 computer.

Many of the tips in this book also apply to the Apple Macintosh, at least in spirit. Backup, Surge Protectors, and Internet safety are still a concern. Viruses and SpyWare are a smaller concern for newer Apple computers.

Topics covered include computer safety and usage tips that should help you and your computer work better today. One cold hard fact is that someday, your computer will die. Let us hope that you have fond memories, rather than curse it for the precious information that it lost upon its demise.

This book was written for you. Every person who has and uses a computer can and must do a little extra to keep that computer working, so that it does not lose its data. Suggestions apply to the family's home computer, as well as to computers in the office at home, the small office environment, and even the larger company (where the staff often assumes that the IT Department can take care of everything).

When something goes wrong with your computer, the problem should be addressed before it gets worse. Often, troubleshooting gets much more difficult when multiple problems exist. So if you have one small problem, solve it right away. Many of the tips in this book can help you avoid problems altogether.

For more information, visit: **www.KeepYourComputerAlive.com**

And Your Sanity Intact

Basic Tips for the Untrained

Most people who use computers are self-taught. Many learn a part of their computer skills through brief classes and seminars. Many people learn tips from friends and family. Skills can be learned from videos, on-line tutorials and books. By far, vocational training classes that favor a self-paced, hands-on approach with the assistance of a knowledgeable instructor provide the most thorough training.

The basic computer skills that you need often do not require a special computer course. But every user is required to learn these basics in order to be able to maintain his or her computer. Here is a quick checklist of these skills:

Control Elements
    Start menu .... A place to initiate nearly every activity
    Control Panel .... Change software and hardware settings
    Windows Explorer .... Manage your computer files

User Functions
    Run a Program .... Pick a program to perform an appropriate activity
    Save a file .... Save the appropriate information
    Copy a file .... Duplicate the information and/or create a backup
    Delete a file .... Remove the information
    Print .... Develop and print meaningful reports from your information

Maintenance Functions
  Turn on and off the computer
  Empty Trash.............. Permanently delete information that was on your computer
  Scan for Viruses........ Safeguard your computer from harmful viruses
  Scan for SpyWare ..... Safeguard your computer from pop-up advertising programs and reduce security risks
  Disk Cleanup............. Automatically remove unnecessary temporary files and empty trash
  Defrag .... Reconnect file fragments to restore your computer efficiency
  Scandisk .... Scan your disk drives for errors and fix them
  Install Software .... Add new program capabilities to your computer
  Uninstall Software..... Remove obsolete or unnecessary programs from your computer
  Backup your data ...... Be prepared for unfortunate computer problems by preparing copies of your information so it can be restored
  Test Uninterruptible Power Supply Battery

Troubleshooting
  My Computer Properties
                    Check Device Manager Properties
  msconfig.................... Disable your startup programs (for Windows 98 or ME)
  regedit .... Display or Edit your register settings
  winipcfg or ipconfig
                    Internet Protocol configuration programs that can assist in troubleshooting network and Internet problems
  Network Places or Network Neighborhood Properties
                    Check network protocols and settings

I am often surprised when I learn that one of my friends does not use the right mouse button. Just click on the right mouse button when "hovering" over a file, button or other object, and you will see a pop-up menu of the options that are available. When you are using your Word Processor or other software, highlight the text, graphic, table or other object on the screen, and use the right mouse button and select the item that you want to use from the pop-up menu. This is much quicker than pulling the mouse back to the top of your page to use the menu or tool buttons.

You don't get reliable computer tips passed on by e-mail. There are many hoaxes.

Terms Used to Describe Windows

The mouse and keyboard are used for most data entries, but other devices can be attached that perform these functions. There are dozens of elements on the screen that serve as visual aids to accomplish tasks. Commonly understood terminology describes these elements.

Many people cannot understand basic computer instructions that are described in verbal terms because they have not learned the names of the graphic elements. When people run into computer trouble, they often cannot follow instructions over the telephone when they reach technical support.

Try to become familiar with the icons and graphics that are associated with the software or device that you are attempting to troubleshoot. Many programs and device drivers become integrated into the Windows system. General program control panel properties become specialized in appearance, once it has been installed.

In order to make your technical support call successful, try to recall every detail of the problem and all information concerning the circumstances.

These graphic elements can be set to appear differently. The user can make the setting changes so that these graphic elements appear in different colors and with different icons. If you use these alternate selections, try to remember how to change these back to the standard Windows setting.

There are appearance differences between versions of Windows. New features were incorporated as a part of a new Microsoft Innovation.

The Task Bar, Icons, Start menu and Program Toolbars can be moved, resized, colored, and modified.

Task Bar - Usually at the bottom of the screen. It contains the Start Button, Quick Launch Tray, Time of Day Clock, specialty items and controls, as well as an Icon for each program that you have running.

Quick Launch Tray - A customizable row of miniature shortcut Icons on the Task Bar.

Start Button - A familiar button marked START; it is found on the Task Bar. This button displays a menu of organized programs and icon shortcuts.

Desktop - The main part of the video display. It may contain Icons, background wallpaper photos or color, Screen Saver and a combination of theme or custom display settings. Right Click on the blank part of the Desktop to view the many customizable setting options.

Icon - A small graphic that is intended to represent a file, folder, program shortcut or other object in your Windows system.

Window - A floating collection object, program or device control that is used to control the operations of a program.

Title Bar - Usually blue, the Title Bar is shown at the top of a Window. It shows the name of the program for that window and may also show the name of the document that is currently open.

Minimize, Maximize, Restore buttons - Usually found on the top right corner of the Title Bar, these buttons control the size of the Window.

And Your Sanity Intact 11

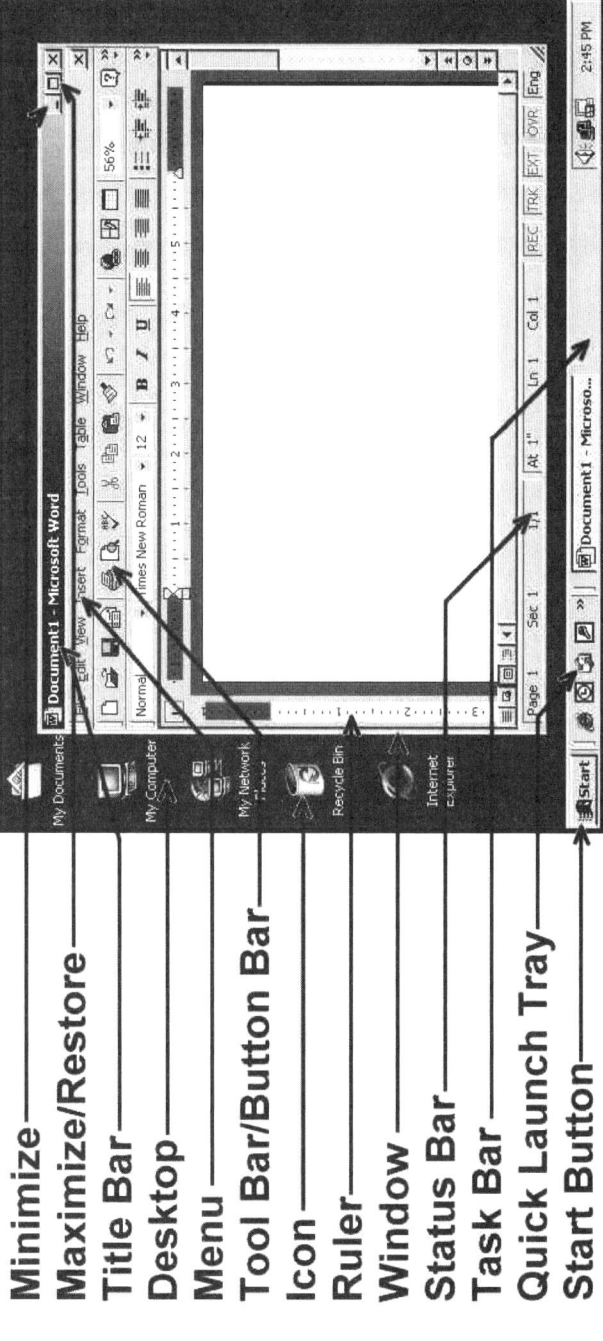

Menu - A menu is a row of text oriented controls near the top of every window. When a Menu item is clicked on, a sub menu appears.

Toolbar, Button Bar - Toolbars contain buttons for providing control of that program.

Ruler - Shown at the top, right, left or bottom of a program, it may provide an indication of how a document may look on paper when printed.

Status Bar - A small row at the bottom of a window, which provides status information concerning that program.

Pop-up Menu - A pop-up menu may appear when the mouse hovers over a specific part of a window, or when the right mouse button is clicked.

Computer Confidence

People generally fear their computers and the possibility that they did something wrong. Hopefully, the problem does not exist between the keyboard and your chair. A positive attitude about your computer and the skills that you are learning will help you gain confidence. Move ahead with confidence and use what you learn to explore still more. The computer maintenance functions are vital to good computer health. You are not the only person who uses your computer. You deliberately allow your computer to be connected to other computers and other people through the Internet. Watch the activities that take place.

Computer software is extremely complex. Many non-fatal errors can occur. In most cases, programs are designed to be extremely fault tolerant, so you might not realize that an error occurred.

Occasionally, an unknown error occurs and an error message is displayed on the screen, which causes the program to stop. You rarely learn about the actual error by an error code. The steps you took to get to that point, are often valuable. You should attempt to recreate the error so that you learn more about how the error was generated.

Surge Protectors & Uninterruptible Power Supply

Undoubtedly, Surge Protectors and Uninterruptible Power Supplies (UPS) can protect your computer. Surge Protectors do not always provide protection against severe lightning, but can help protect your computer from minor power line fluctuations that are caused by your refrigerator or air conditioner. Uninterruptible Power Supplies work a great deal better than Surge Protectors, but require regular maintenance and a new battery from time to time. The third option is owning a Power Conditioner.

A Power Conditioner can provide power interruption protection against 90% of the brown-out and "lights flickering" events that occur without the regular replacement cost of the batteries in a UPS. The home computer user probably does not need complete power interruption protection but can benefit greatly with a Power Conditioner that requires no maintenance.

Both Power Conditioners and UPSs do not guarantee equipment protection against the most severe electrical storms, so home computers should be turned off when these potentially damaging storms arise. For life supplying equipment in hospitals, important computer equipment is protected with backup generators and high technology transient suppression equipment, such as the Stabiline series that is manufactured by Superior Electric in Connecticut.

Your electrician can install transient suppression equipment that protects your whole house. Your electric utility may offer this service.

Keep in mind that lightning may enter your computer through telephone lines.

Viruses and Anti-Virus

Obviously, there is a war between computer software manufacturers and a large underground of virus writers. Viruses are software designed to cause problems in the efficient operation of specific computer functions. Viruses have plagued computers from the earliest days. There is no computer that is completely isolated from this problem. In fact, any computer that is on the Internet and does not have anti-virus software has a virus.

I have had the best success with Norton Antivirus software. There are a number of good providers of anti-virus solutions.

Many people are confused with the terms "What Version" and "Getting Updates". If you have the Norton Antivirus 2003 version, that means you have the software that was released in 2003. This does not mean that it does not work, but a newer version is available.

When you first install Norton Antivirus, it comes with a one-year subscription of the Virus Definition Updates. That means that you can go on-line and get updates either automatically, or manually by using the LIVE UPDATE feature. When using the manual method, you may also get some program updates that have been released by this manufacturer.

When your update subscription expires, there are two ways that you can extend your subscription. The first is to use the on-line method to purchase the subscription renewal. The second is to purchase the new version of Anti-virus software. I prefer the second method, since I will then own the disk of the software. I do not assume that my computer will live through the year, and hope that I can reinstall this and other software on the replacement drive, should something go wrong. You might be planning on buying a new computer next year, so it would not make any difference. It can be cheaper to buy the updates on-line.

Your computer should be scanned completely for viruses on a weekly basis. Begin this process during a time when the computer is not in use because the computer will run slowly during the scan. Many Anti-virus programs can be set to run automatically.

Your Anti-virus software has a status window that will tell you when the subscription expires; when the last updates were downloaded and installed; and when the last full system scan has occurred. Look at this status window on a regular basis to ensure that everything is progressing as planned. Many users are simply unaware that this process has stopped, so their computers became infected anyway.

You should have only ONE Anti-virus software program installed on your computer. These types of programs do not play well together.

For more information about Norton Antivirus, check their website at **www.symantec.com/nav/nav_pro**.

I know people who have opened e-mail attachments, ignored the anti-virus software warnings and become infected with viruses.

Viruses are designed to pass the infection from one computer to another. Only an infected computer will pass viruses on. If everyone were protected and savvy about this issue, viruses could become obsolete.

The Windows product has a large market share. While it comes in a number of flavors, it is easy for people to learn. But the authors of viruses also have an advantage when they attack the Windows computer. They have a larger target audience. Because of this advantage, I recommend that the world market should encourage the development of a wide diversity of computer environments and operating systems. A single source of anti-virus software would not make our global network immune. I suggest that multiple anti-virus solutions be encouraged to keep an active diversity of solutions and protection. A large number of different computer environments provide a larger challenge to the authors of virus software.

SpyWare and Pop-up Ads

SpyWare is software that is installed on your computer without your knowledge or intention. It appears after visiting a website that is less reputable or not the one you intended. Often, SpyWare appears as an add-on software or as setting changes to your Web browser. It is called SpyWare because this software begins to run on its own and is aware when you connect to the Internet. It then makes every effort to deliver pop-up windows and advertisements to you. The real problem with SpyWare is when you get TOO MUCH. I have seen dozens of these programs running on an infected computer.

Programs like SpyBot Search & Destroy and Ad-aware were written to seek out and remove these programs. These anti-SpyWare programs also include an update feature and status report. They cannot be set to run automatically. You must run them periodically to keep your computer clean.

While you can have more than one Anti-SpyWare software program installed on your computer, usually one will do. You will find a favorite and grow to rely on it.

When you see unusual add-on programs on your computer or web browser, I recommend that you check the Add/Remove Programs section of your Control Panel and use the correct procedure to un-install these programs. Then run Ad-aware or SpyBot to look for other SpyWare programs.

Your browser's home page is the setting of the website that appears when you open it for the first time. When your home page has been changed, you should suspect a SpyWare problem. You should use the Internet Settings function of the Control Panel to reset your home page. Many computers have this set to **http://www.msn.com**

Learn more about Ad-aware at the following website: **www.lavasoftusa.com.**

For information about SpyBot Search & Destroy, check their website at **spybot.safer-networking.de/en**.

SpyWare can be avoided by using Mozilla FireFox to browse the Internet instead of Internet Explorer. Visit **www.mozilla.org** for this free download.

Without changing their browsing habits, people have re-infected their computers with SpyWare a few days after correcting the problem. Do not visit websites that persistently cause pop-up ads.

Firewalls

Many people are mystified with firewalls. There are a number of different kinds, along with a wide variety of software programs that are intended to protect your computer from outside intrusion. The best firewall solution is one that allows easy access to the websites of choice, and unwanted websites are blocked. The confusing part comes when the user does not understand how to UNBLOCK the websites they want, and can still set blocks against the unwanted sites.

Firewalls can be used to prevent SpyWare and Pop-up Ads.

My personal favorite firewall is the one that is included in a DSL/Cable Router. The advantage of this firewall is that a single point of control can protect a number of computers on the same network. Then I do not have to worry about the software firewall failing or getting corrupted.

The most popular software firewall solution is ZoneAlarm. This is available on-line as well as at your local stationary or computer store. Visit their website at **www.zonelabs.com**.

Whenever you have trouble with your Internet connection for viewing websites or getting your e-mail, try disabling your firewall temporarily to see if the connection is being blocked.

Avoid using public Hot Spot wireless locations to initiate secure transactions. These locations are great for looking up sport scores, news, weather and other information, but are inappropriate for logging into your bank account or shopping on-line.

File Sharing

Keep your computer safe by turning off all file sharing.

Use Windows Explorer to look for file sharing. Any folder where file sharing is enabled is shown with a small blue hand under the yellow folder icon.

When you discover that a folder is SHARED, use the right mouse button and pick SHARING from the menu. Click on the checkbox to disable sharing.

If you use a music download program like Napster, Kazaa or Warez, be sure to disable file sharing when you are not using it. Always watch the progress of any file downloads when using these programs. Close these programs when you have completed your downloads. Reactivate your Firewall if you disabled it.

Any download program that uses "Peer to Peer file sharing" (P2P) poses a security risk to your computer. Always be aware of the file types for files that you are downloading from websites or attached to e-mails. File types are best recognized by the 3 or 4 letter file extension that appears to the right of the period in the file name.

Typical File Types

Executable or Script files ***
.exe, .com, .bat, .vbs

Documents, Spreadsheets, Presentation, Database **
.doc, .xls, .ppt, .mdb, .dbf, .txt, .asc, .wri

Graphics & Pictures *
.jpg, .gif, .png, .bmp

Music & Sound *
.mp3, .wma, .mid, .wav

Video *
.mpg, .mpe, .wmv

Compressed or Zip files ** (depending on its contents and origin)
.zip

Internet
.htm, .html, .asp, .cgi, .php., xml

*** .... high risk
** .... medium risk
* .... low risk

32 *Keep Your Computer Alive*

Children Use Computers

Computer problems get worse, faster, when you share your computer with children. Children are nearly fearless and very curious. While they seem to know and learn more about your computer, they also fail to realize the importance of simple security and maintenance procedures. They often get bored and walk away from a computer when problems begin to arise.

Establish family rules. Insist that children check the Anti-Virus and Anti-SpyWare software. Ensure that File Sharing and downloading is done safely. Do not allow download files of just any type.

Use a firewall to block specific websites. Use the CONTENT ADVISOR feature of Internet Explorer. From the Control Panel, select the INTERNET OPTIONS. Then click on the CONTENT Tab, then Set and Enable the Content Advisor password. While it may be time consuming at first to approve many websites, this will control what websites your youngsters visit.

Children should not reveal personal information about themselves on-line without a parent's permission. This includes their name, e-mail address, postal address, phone number, photo, school address, social security number, etc. Children should be taught to report any attempt to contact them to their parents or teachers.

Other children and adults posing as children can be very cruel to each other in chat rooms. Remember that users can be anonymous on-line, and use anything for a screen name. They can also use alternate identities. Parents must monitor their chat room activities. Your child may become a target of an on-line attack. Watch for attitude and changes in self-esteem. Help your children to learn more and use their identity wisely.

Visit **kids.getnetwise.org** for more information.

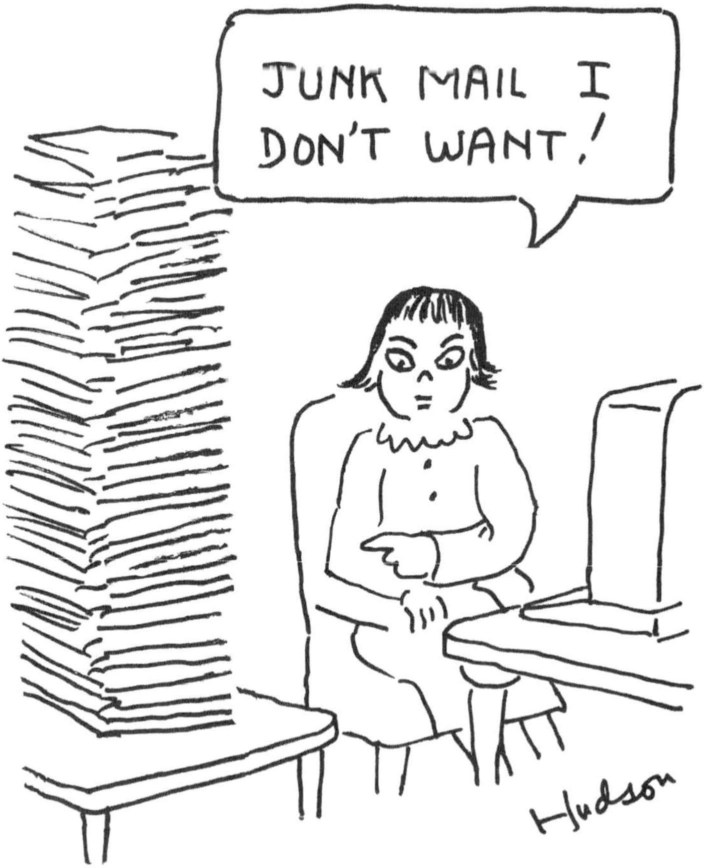
JUNK MAIL I DON'T WANT!
Hudson

Avoid SPAM

Unsolicited e-mail has become so prevalent that people with a brand new e-mail address begin to get SPAM right away. The only way to avoid this problem is to start taking measures to avoid it. I have some accounts that receive over 1,000 SPAM messages per day. Certainly, I take steps to minimize the amount of time that I spend managing this problem.

Yes, you should show an E-mail address on your website. This address must be one that you can change. What would be the point of having a website with no way for someone to contact you electronically?

If you have a website, use an e-mail alias. Consider a displayed address as Temporary. This address would be set up to forward e-mail to your regular e-mail address. Eventually, that e-mail address will attract too much SPAM. When the SPAM increases again, you can select a different alias. Use an address such as info@myDomain.com or response@myDomain.com

Maintain a free web-based e-mail address, such as Hotmail or Yahoo for registering products. Check this e-mail just to REPORT and Delete SPAM. These free services work hard to avoid SPAM. Test this address regularly to ensure that the service still works; so that when you DO use it, it does work. If it stops working, simply get another e-mail address and test it before using it.

Tell your friends to NEVER register your e-mail address on any website. This means DO NOT send me an on-line greeting card. DO NOT use the on-line group member feature to invite me to join the on-line group. DO NOT use a website's feature to invite me to see your on-line photos. Tell them specifically that your e-mail address is PRIVATE. If they do wish to share something with you, they can e-mail you directly first. At this point, you would give them permission, along with the TEMPORARY e-mail address that you use for this purpose.

Send or Forward e-mail to a large list of e-mail addresses using the BCC field. (BCC refers to Blind Carbon Copy). You should not be sharing other people's e-mail addresses with the whole group. Do not use REPLY ALL, unless you know that everyone already knows everyone else and you really want everyone to have the reply. You should not multiply the originator's mistake.

Most e-mail programs have a REPLY ALL button. It would be great if all e-mail addresses were copied to the BCC field when this button is used.

You should be careful when you Report SPAM. Try not to report your friends by mistake. This may hurt their electronic communications. If your friend is sending you TOO MANY jokes and other e-mail, just ask them to STOP.

While SPAM blocking tools and E-mail approval software works well, it is best to simply avoid SPAM, rather than ignore it. At some point, your SPAM or BULK folder will have too much e-mail in it.

I do recommend that you own a Domain Name that can forward specific e-mail addresses to your regular e-mail INBOX. One or more names can be your Permanent Alias, and others can be your Temporary Alias; which can be forwarded to the Permanent address if you wish. Not all Domain Name providers perform this service.

If your e-mail address is reported as SPAM by others, be sure to use an alternate e-mail address to contact those people.

The only way that the Internet can continue to work for everyone is more education about the simple Rules of the Road. People will FLOCK away from the Internet, or not use their e-mail if the SPAM problem continues. Let's all work to make the Internet a useful tool.

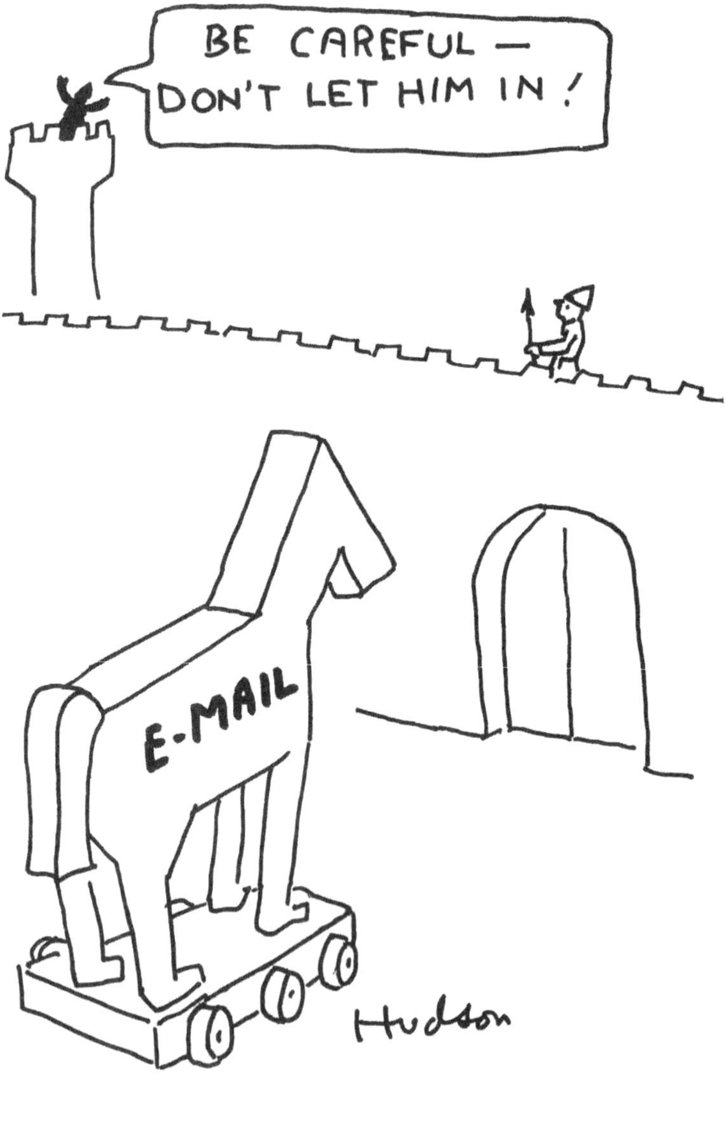
BE CAREFUL — DON'T LET HIM IN!
E-MAIL
Hudson

Be Careful Opening E-mail

Viruses, Worms and SpyWare get into your computer by a number of means, but most often via e-mail. File attachments, as well as formatted e-mail can deliver scripts that open security holes and deliver the main attack into your computer.

These e-mails can appear to come from someone that you know. But they could be coming from someone else's infected computer. This is known as "Spoofing". There are some telltale signs.

1. E-mail subject line is blank or out of character
2. Full or characteristic name is not shown with e-mail address
3. Message is terse and out of character
4. Deliberately misspelled words
5. Attachment is of an unusual file type

Do not open unknown or uncharacteristic e-mail messages.

Here are some tips in making your e-mail more characteristic, so people know that it is from you.

1. When you send out e-mail, your e-mail setting should show a name. Mine says "Daniel A. Uitti" with my e-mail address.
2. Always use a subject line that refers to a known subject between you and the recipient.
3. Always mention the recipient's name in the message section of the e-mail.
4. Always type your name at the closing of the message.

5. Write e-mail in a more formal manner, instead of in a short and non-descriptive manner. For example: don't say just "OK".
6. Describe the attached file, and what program should open it properly.
7. Use an E-mail signature that identifies you.
8. When passing along jokes or trivial messages, ADD the words "Joke" or "Fun Facts" to the subject.

Using this improved e-mail etiquette will help everyone see and realize when a message is important and authentic.

You can receive e-mail that appears to come from a bank, PayPal or eBay. The e-mail message suggests that you log into their website to verify your account or recent order. The message suggests that you "click" on the message to Login. Never click on the link that appears in the message. This is spoof e-mail and/or an attempt at Identity Theft. These institutions would not use e-mail to inform you of a serious login or verification problem.

Go to their website through your browser. Look for the problem that was discussed in the suspect e-mail. You will probably discover that the e-mail was fraudulent, or an attempt at Identity Theft. If you did login through the e-mail, the thief may have just learned your login and password. Contact the real organization immediately by logging into their real website and change your password immediately.

One of my friends received a spoof e-mail from eBay. The next day, his account was being used to sell Motorcycle Parts. It is safe to assume that the identity thief was trying to steal from another unsuspecting buyer.

Most of these institutions would like to hear about spoof e-mails. For eBay messages, you can forward these to **spoof@eBay.com**. For PayPal, you can forward these to **spoof@PayPal.com**.

And Your Sanity Intact 41

Backup Your Data

You should have the Restore Disks that came with your computer. You should have the Software Disks of every program that you have purchased and installed. This set of disks will be needed someday when your computer needs drastic repair. It might need a new hard disk drive. It might become so infected with Viruses and/or SpyWare that it will not run, and cannot be restored without starting over.

For the user, there is a distinct advantage to having a properly licensed copy of every software program on your computer. At some point, that software will have to be reinstalled on your computer when you have a problem and you will need that original disk again. If a software package costs too much, simply select a different program that will do the same thing.

Software is installed and not Backed Up. When you have to restore the computer, software must be reinstalled.

Organize your data in a manner that is logical. Most software encourages you to store data files in the "My Documents" folder. But some software has a special "data" folder in it's own "Program Files" section. This is especially true for software from Quicken, Quickbooks, and a number of accounting software packages. Older versions of WordPerfect stored files elsewhere also. These files can be MOVED to folders in your "My Documents" folder.

While there are a number of BACK UP programs, many computers come with a CD-Burner and the software necessary to create CDs. These are very simple to use, and often take less then 10 minutes to create.

For easy access to your backups, using the standard COPY function from Windows Explorer is enough. Good, sophisticated backup software that tracks changes to files and stores only updated files is very good for small businesses, but this software is fairly expensive.

Keep in mind that if you do not backup your data someday you will lose it.

Accounting programs like Quickbooks do provide a built-in backup feature. It is important to know that you should have more than one set of disks that you back up to regularly. You never know when the set of backup disks that you use will suddenly stop working, leaving you without a backup.

If your information is critical, consider storing the backup set in a different location.

Windows ME and Windows XP come with a System Restore facility. If you have Windows 98 or Windows 2000, you might consider buying Norton GoBack. This came with a number of computer brands, including Gateway.

For more information on Norton GoBack, check their website at **www.symantec.com/goback**.

If you have a fairly new computer with a very large hard drive, you might consider using a software product like Norton Ghost. This product will use a part of your hard drive to duplicate your main hard drive and make fast and complete backup and restorations possible.

For more information on Norton Ghost, check their website at **www.symantec.com/ghost**.

Many people will discover that their computers have stopped working and they do not have a recent backup.

YOUR BACKUP SHOULD BE IN GOOD SHAPE FOR THE LONG HAUL!

Backup Media

During the course of 25 years of microcomputers, media for storing information for that tiny computer has changed many times. The IBM PC became a standard that captured a significant market share. When focusing just on the IBM PC platform and its derivatives, you can see a migration from 5¼ inch floppy disk to 3½ inch floppy disk, Iomega Zip disks, a variety of backup tape drives, CD-ROM/DVD Media and today's USB Flash Memory Sticks. Backward compatibility to the older media types is not guaranteed.

Data is not guaranteed to be safe on many of the older magnetic media types. It seems that the CD-ROM will provide very long-term data storage. The CD-R media has an expected life of 50 years. The CD-RW media may have a shorter life. Floppy diskettes may begin to degrade and lose the information in ten years, and can cease to function at any time.

Many new computers today do not come with a 3½ inch floppy disk drive. If you need this to install your backup data, be sure to buy one.

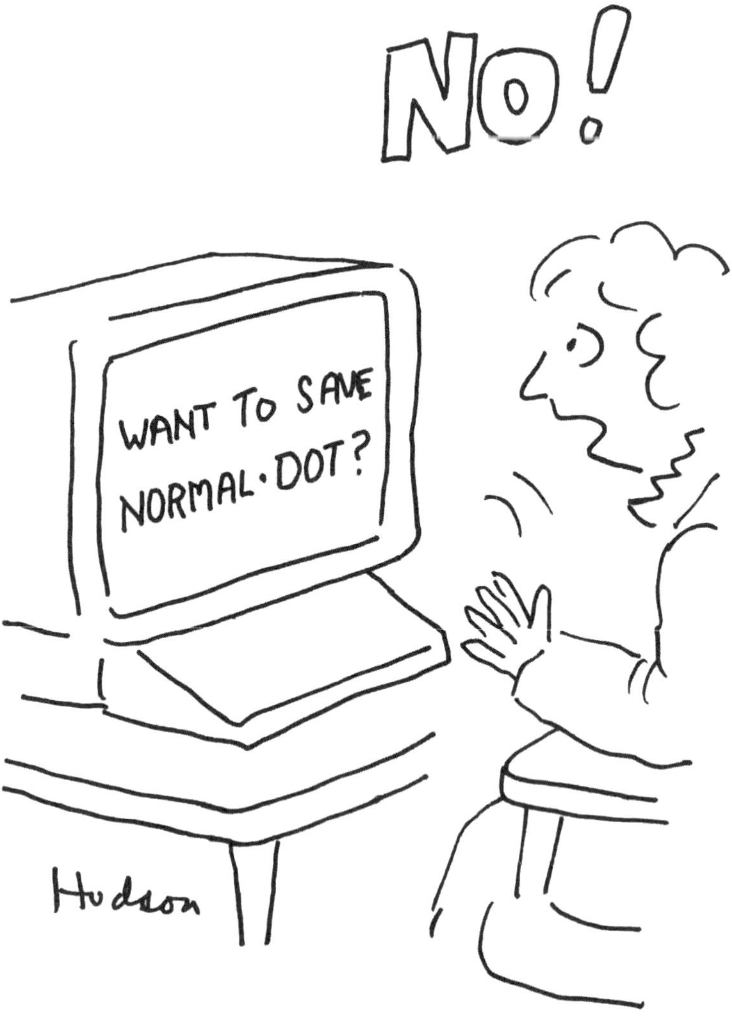
NO!
WANT TO SAVE
NORMAL.DOT?
Hudson

Save While You Work

People who have been using computers for ten years or more know instinctively that computers might freeze-up or crash at any minute. They have developed a sense of when to save and save again. But computers run much more reliably today, and newcomers put themselves at risk to lose their data.

I recommend that you use the SAVE button, or select SAVE from the FILE menu as you work. The programs that have a SAVE feature may or may not have a working automatic save feature that is dependable. So if this feature is available, then use it. I use the Save button whenever I have typed in a complete thought; or about every ten minutes.

Many programs work on a transaction basis and save the data for you automatically. Every time you create an invoice or checkbook entry, the data is saved. Other programs will perform an automatic backup as you work. Should you close the program suddenly or lose power to your computer, you may not have lost any of your work.

Occasionally, Microsoft Word will ask you if you want to save changes to Normal.dot. To this question, always say NO. This is the start-up template file and not your document. Keep in mind that the "doc" file extension means Document; and the "dot" file extension means template.

From the Tools Menu of Windows Explorer, you can see that Microsoft allows you to HIDE the three-character file extension of known file types. This is the normal setting of Windows Explorer. I see no benefit from hiding this fact. Instead, I believe that the user should always know and see that this is a part of a file name, and it should not be hidden.

The word DEFAULT is associated by most people as a way to describe when a loan payment has not been made. When used with computers, default indicates the original setting or the standard setting.

And Your Sanity Intact   49

Restore Your Computer

There are several levels of Restore on the computer today. Every effort should be made to know the status of your backup copies and which restore options you need to use.

Windows ME and Windows XP come with a Restore Point utility program that allows you to Create a Restore Point and to Restore from a Restore Point. This is a calendar-based tool, which guides you to restoring the program registrations and settings to a known good state. Try to remember when you first see problems so that you can take advantage of this feature.

Your computer probably came with Restore Disks. These disks are the fastest way to correct the most severe problems. Some manufacturers provide restore disks that contain two methods of restoration. One level will attempt to restore parts of the operating system without destroying your data. The second level will erase the entire hard drive and install the original software to return your computer to a refreshed, new state.

What is important to know right now is: WHERE ARE THOSE DISKS? You should locate those disks, along with other software that you want to be able to reinstall on your computer, and store them in one location. I recommend that you place them together in a single resealable bag or box.

Some computer manufacturers do not provide you with a set of Restore disks. Check the manual to see if you are supposed to buy these separately. Other computer manufactures provide you with a method to BURN YOUR OWN restore set. This should be done as soon as you buy the computer since it might be damaged soon after you install other software. This special BURN YOUR OWN program is designed to operate only once. Be sure to have plenty of CD-R disks before you start.

And Your Sanity Intact 51

Write Down Passwords & Registration Numbers

This sounds pretty silly. If you keep a file on your computer with all of your passwords and software registration numbers on your computer, and it dies, how do you recover this information?

Obviously, you should write down all login names, passwords, account numbers and software registration numbers in a notebook or on a piece of paper, so that if your computer dies; you can access these accounts again when you get a new computer.

I do not recommend using a password saving program. One such program delivers advertising to your computer. This same program is blocked by anti-SpyWare software such as Ad-aware.

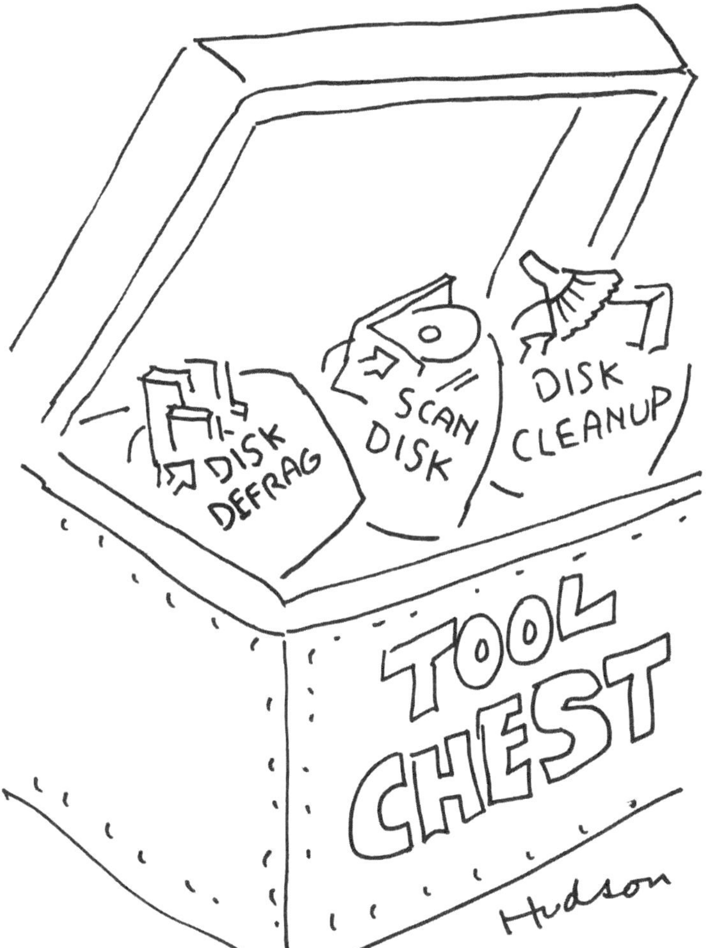
DISK DEFRAG
SCAN DISK
DISK CLEANUP
TOOL CHEST
Hudson

Scandisk, Defrag & Disk Cleanup

These three software tools have been a part of the Windows system since the beginning, yet people have purchased third party software to accomplish the same thing. I have not used third party software such as this since the days of MS-DOS.

Windows 2000 and Windows XP were designed around a resilient hard drive formatting technology. The use of scandisk and defrag programs is less important for this new technology. Some performance increase may be realized by using these maintenance tools every few months, instead of weekly or monthly.

If you have Windows 2000 or Windows XP, look for the Disk Defragmenter in the Programs section, under Accessories and System Tools sections. The Scandisk feature is accessed by Right Clicking on the drive that you wish to test, and picking Properties in the pop-up menu. Click on the TAB that is marked "Tools". Click on the button that says "Test Now". Active drives under Windows 2000 & Windows XP must be tested after re-starting the computer. While you can test the active drive in Windows 98 and Windows ME, it is more efficient to restart the computer into Safe Mode and run scandisk.

Safe Mode is an important troubleshooting feature of Windows, but many devices and programs are disabled while in that mode. Restart the computer and watch the monitor very carefully as the computer restarts. You must tap the "F8" key on the keyboard at some point before the familiar light blue Windows screen appears. The timing is important, and easily missed. A black menu appears, which provides you with a list of restart options. Safe Mode appears in that list. Use the down arrow key on your keyboard to pick Safe Mode, or type the option number.

Disk Cleanup is a simple program that is supplied with all versions of Windows. It appears in the System folder, in the Accessories section of your Programs. I recommend that you use the Disk Cleanup program prior to running Defrag and Scandisk. You should not use the TRASH folder to store information that you might need.

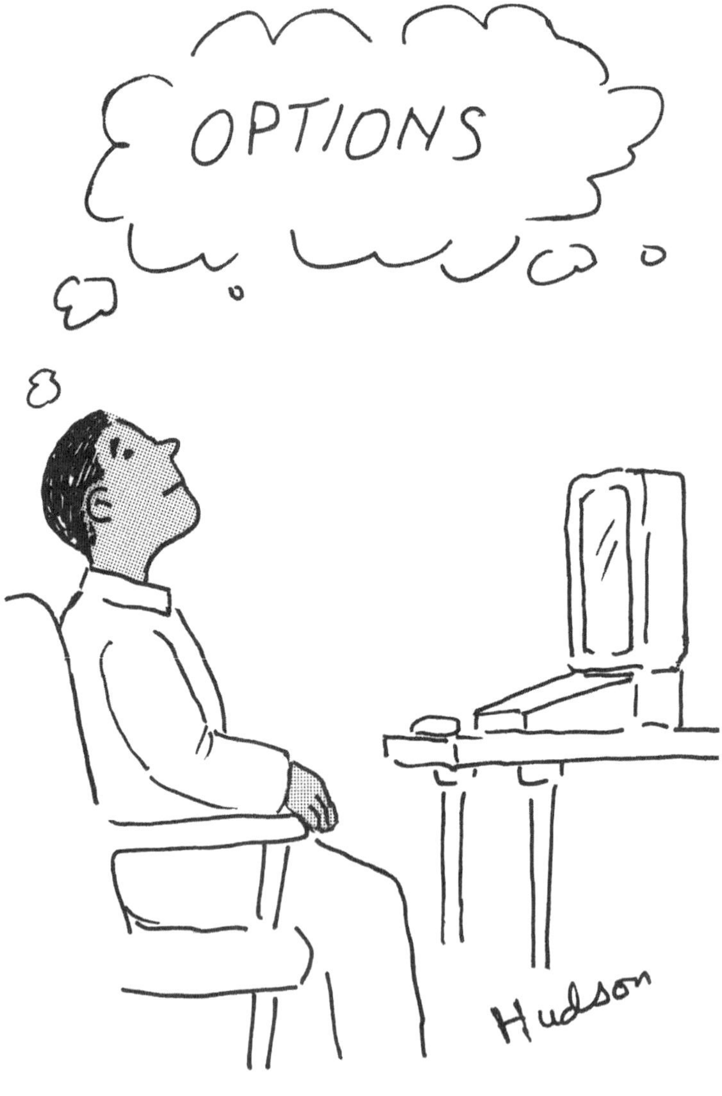
OPTIONS
Hudson

What Should I Install on My Computer?

Don't think of your computer in the same manner that you do a refrigerator, microwave oven or can opener. None of those devices are expandable to any extent. Your computer is more comparable to the whole kitchen. Imagine a kitchen with components that come from all different manufacturers. My own kitchen contains nearly all Whirlpool appliances. But your computer has Kitchen-aid, GE, Sunbeam, Amana, Mr. Coffee and many other brand names, all within the same box. Almost any one of these branded parts or software packages can be replaced by a different brand. The combinations of hardware and software are endless. Some mixes of components might not work.

It is because of this complexity that I recommend that you buy and install only those software programs and components that you need. If your computer is used to help you run a small business, and you need your computer on an increasing basis, then do not install games or non-essential devices.

If you purchase a disk that contains a collection of fonts, be sure to install only the fonts that you are going to use. Do not attempt to remove any of the fonts that were originally installed on your computer. I recommend that you never install more then 400 fonts on your computer. Many programs take longer to startup when you have too many fonts installed.

Many new computers come with a number of software programs that you don't need. After you have determined their function, you might want to use the Add/Remove section of the Control Panel to uninstall these programs.

Many people have more than one computer and dedicate one of their computers for their work. When possible, first install new software on the computer that is not critical for your business. Test this software and all of the other software that you normally use. Then you can install this new software on your business-oriented computer with higher confidence. In spite of the claim, new software may not work well with every possible combination of computer and software.

Be sure to review the system requirements of the new software. Be sure that you know how much disk space is required, how much memory is required and all other software prerequisites. If you are using Windows 2000, be sure that your operating system is specifically listed. Do not assume that it might work on your computer.

Computer Essentials

Take the time to decide what business functions will be performed by your computer. Organize and design your processes. Do not use your computer by mistake, but rather as a deliberate time and cost saving device. Here are some of the essential computer software programs for Internet use.

> Windows Update
> RealOne Player
> Windows Media Player
> QuickTime Player
> Anti-Virus Software
> Anti-SpyWare Software
> Word Processor
> Special Internet Software as required by your Internet provider
> Mozilla Firefox
> Adobe Acrobat Reader
> Macromedia Flash

Software Updates

As previously mentioned, anti-virus and anti-SpyWare updates are good and necessary to be vigilant against the newest threats. Updating tax tables for accounting software helps keep your payroll accounting calculations up to date when you are using the automated feature.

Be skeptical. Many software programs include update capabilities. Can you download these program updates all the time? Can you make a backup of these program updates, so you can return your computer to the current working state? Do some of these updates cause more problems than they fix?

Whenever updating your Windows software, using the Windows Update feature, be skeptical. Read the description of those updates. Do you have a plan if the update that you are downloading ruins your computer? Are you prepared for an unscheduled computer maintenance cycle, if the update does not work?

Are you sharing data with other people, and does the update retain data compatibility with the previous version?

If your computer is stable and performing the tasks that you require, think twice before introducing a software update. "If it ain't broke, don't fix it."

Major software updates, such as an upgrade from Windows ME to Windows XP, may prove to work out poorly for your computer, since it was designed to work with Windows ME. Windows XP requires a more powerful computer.

Hardware Updates

A modest amount of money can be spent that will enhance the speed and capacity of your computer. Most new computers come with all that you need. Computers are designed to run efficiently for a specific Operating System and version. So if your computer came with Windows ME, I recommend that you stay with that. Installing Windows XP will only make your computer run slower. The best way to get increased performance is to add Memory. Unfortunately, it comes in many specifications, and it is difficult to find the exact memory for your computer. Purchasing this memory from the manufacturer can be a slow and expensive process. You can buy memory that "might work" from a national stationary store that has a good return policy. Then just try it, and bring it back if it does not work. The other approach is to check with an on-line memory company that shows your make and model in their "look up" feature. One such website is **CoastMemory.com**.

I know people who purchased a larger hard drive instead of more memory, after getting an error message that stated that Memory is Low. Programs that you run use memory temporarily. Disk space is used to store your programs and data for the long term. When sufficient memory is not available, some disk space is used temporarily as memory, but your computer operates much slower. For additional performance, more memory is needed and not disk space.

And Your Sanity Intact

Where Do These Wires Go?

Even a problem like "No Sound" can be tricky to troubleshoot.

Did the computer get moved? When did you hear the sound work last? Did you install new software?

Check the Control Panel, then go to the SYSTEM section and click on the TAB marked "HARDWARE" (or Device Manager). Then click on Device Manager. Is there a Yellow or Red flag showing for the Audio device?

Go back to the Control Panel and open the SOUND section. Is there a checkbox to show the Sound Control on the Task Bar? You should see a little yellow loudspeaker on the Task Bar near the clock. Try picking one of the Sound Events and Click the PLAY button.

The speakers can be plugged into one of three possible locations. On most computers, it is the light green jack.

Video Cable - It is usually blue. It is a D-Shaped connector that has 15 pins, organized in three rows. This connector usually has thumbscrews. Before connecting it, be sure the computer and the monitor power are turned off.

Printer Cable - This cable is usually Gray or Black. If this is not a USB cable, it is then a D-Shaped connector with 25 pins that are arranged in two rows. This connector usually has thumbscrews. This connector should not be reconnected when the computer or printer power are turned on.

Ethernet or Network cable - This connector is a snap-in style connector that appears very similar to a telephone connector. It is somewhat wider and will not fit into your telephone modem. It has 8 pins.

Telephone Wire - This connector is a snap-in style connector. It appears to have the capacity to hold six connections, but usually has two or four. Your modem usually has two telephone jacks. The wire from the wall connects into the jack that is marked with the word "Wall" or shows a picture of a telephone jack. It is often color coded green. The other jack is marked with the word "Phone" or shows a picture of a telephone. You may plug a telephone handset, FAX machine or other telephone system device into this jack.

Keyboard - This connector is usually small and round. Some manufacturers color code this orange or purple. The connector must be rotated to align it correctly into the jack on the computer. The computer usually shows a picture of a keyboard near this connector, or color codes it to match the keyboard.

Mouse - The Mouse connector is usually small and round. Most manufacturers color code this green. The connector must be rotated to align it correctly into the jack on the computer. The jack on the computer may also be green, or show a picture of a mouse.

USB - There are many devices that can be plugged into your computer through USB connectors. Many can be plugged in while the computer is turned on. These devices can probably be used right away without restarting the computer.

You can purchase a USB hub to expand the number of USB connectors that you have on your computer. But complex devices may not work through the hub. If a printer also has a built-in Flash Card reader, then it may not work through a hub. Many USB based network or wireless network adapters also will not work through a hub.

The more complex devices often work best when connected to the USB port that it was first plugged into when the software was installed for that device.

Moving a Computer

Before moving your computer, be sure to review the locations of each wire and plug. Remove all diskettes and CDs. Carefully organize your CDs so that you keep your important programs and backup disks. Try to use the original containers for your computer and its components. Locate and organize all of the documentation. Box all of the smaller components together. Mark your cables and power strips with shipping labels when you are not sure of what they are and where they go.

When you first set up your computer, start with the basics first. Your keyboard, mouse and monitor are the crucial components. You can test your new computer setup with just those components at first. Then turn your computer off again and add your printer and other devices.

If your computer seems to be DEAD after the move, but you hear a repeating beep, some circuit cards may have come lose during your move. Remove the power cords, and then remove the cover from the computer tower. Carefully press each of the removable circuit cards to ensure that they are in tight. Carefully press on each of the ribbon cable connectors that you see as well. Then you can replace the cover and plug it in again.

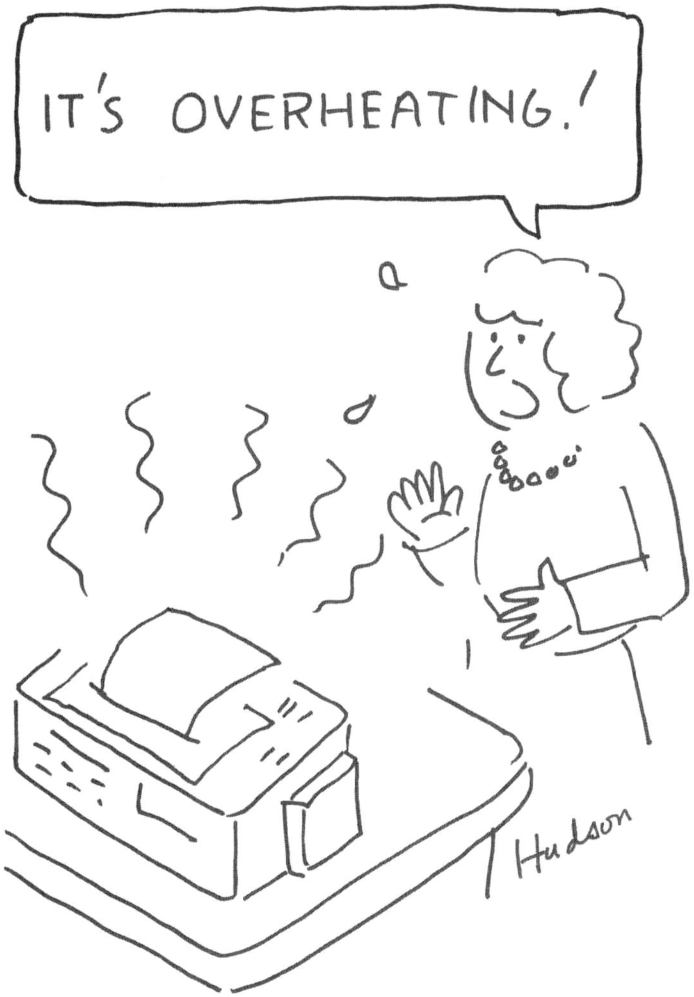
IT'S OVERHEATING!
Hudson

Keeping Your Printer in Top Shape

Be sure to read the manual that came with your printer. There are some cleaning and maintenance tips. Many printers meet their end when they can no longer feed paper properly. This is often caused by repeated paper jams, where jammed paper has finally damaged the mechanism. An excess of ink or toner causes other fatal problems.

In many cases, Inkjet manufacturers recommend that you should only purchase ink from them. While you can save money by refilling cartridges yourself, or by buying generic cartridges, you might not get as much service from this cheaper method. When using these alternatives, check for the buildup of ink inside the printer. Try to keep track of the number of pages that are actually printed.

Laser printers run quite hot. They are not designed to run continuously. Manufacturers rate their laser printers by the number of copies per month. Even this does not mean that you can print 200 page documents all at once. For personal laser printers, I recommend that you print under a dozen pages at a time; then allow the printer to cool for 5 minutes before continuing the large printout. You might control printing a large printout session by putting only a dozen sheets of paper into the paper tray, and allowing it to run out. Then resume the printing by adding another dozen sheets.

When you simply send out a 100 or so page printout, you will find that the toner will be applied to the paper with too much heat. The toner can then stick to the paper feeding rollers and jam up the machine. The repair costs are simply too high to take this risk. If you really do expect to print hundred page reports on a regular basis, check the ratings of the printer that you intend to buy.

Color laser printers are even more susceptible to damage by overheating. These printers are too expensive to replace or repair; so use caution when printing a large run. I would probably restrict printing to no more than 6 at a time. I would watch the printer before, during and after printing to look for toner buildup; feel the heat given off from new printed pages; and smell the printer to learn if something might have a burning odor.

With all printers, you will find that the paper feed mechanism will work better with a specific brand or weight of paper. If a particular brand jams in the machine regularly, then buy a heavier weight paper or a better brand. As a printer gets older, it gets even fussier about the paper that it will feed. I have found that many small inkjet printers like a 24-pound weight paper and dislike standard copy machine paper.

You will find many of the same issues with personal copy machines. Many will print just 10 copies before getting too hot to work properly. Even though the dial says that you can make 100 or more, keep your copy count down to a modest number. It is very easy to burn out a brand new copying machine.

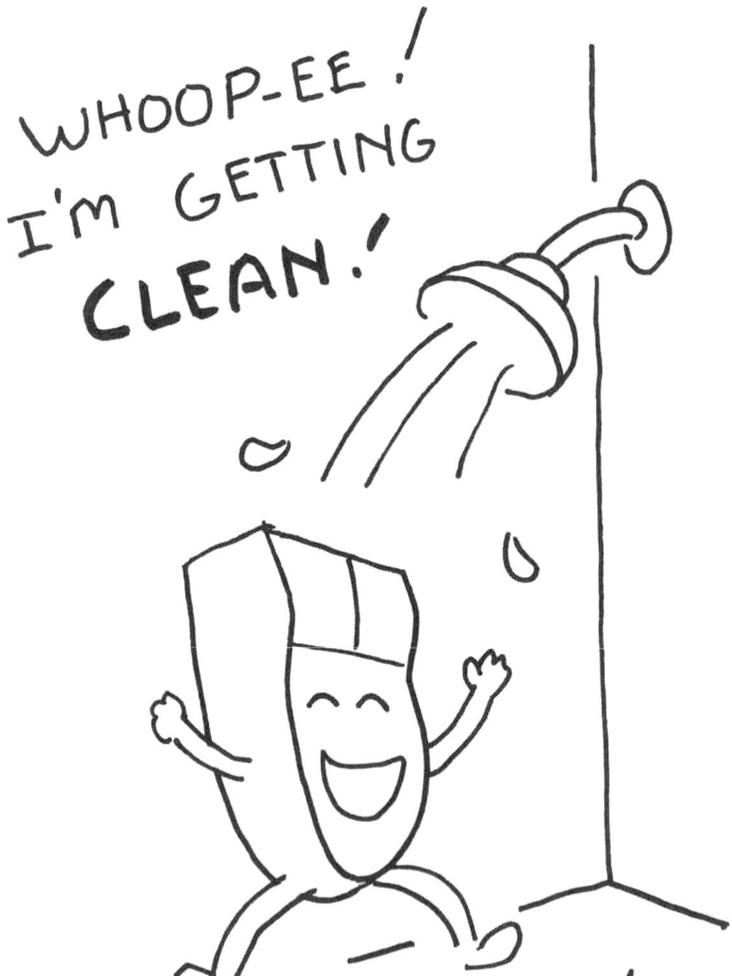
WHOOP-EE!
I'M GETTING
CLEAN!
Hudson

Controlling that Wild Mouse

Many people have minor problems in controlling the mouse. While a computer is not a toy, and I do not recommend playing GAMES, new users should take some time to play the Solitaire game. This helps to improve dexterity and teaches skills like DOUBLE CLICK and DRAG and DROP.

At some point, however, the ball inside the mouse drags dust and such into the roller mechanisms. Some manuals and user guides suggest that you clean the ball. But it is not the ball that is dirty. It is the miniature rollers inside the mouse that have collected the grime.

To clean the mouse, you want to remove the ball. Then use your fingernail or small nail file to carefully scrape the dust and other material that builds up on the rollers inside the mouse. Roll the roller to ensure that it is completely clean.

A mouse fails for two reasons. The first is that the rollers have become too dirty to clean. The second is that the wire that connects it to the computer has shorted or broken.

I recommend that you get an Optical mouse. This means that you will not have to clean it. These do not require a mouse pad; but you certainly can use one. (A mouse pad reserves the appropriate amount of space on your desk).

Some people have a little trouble with a wireless optical mouse. While it seems that the wireless mouse would solve both failure types that I mentioned above, it is heavier than a corded mouse because of the weight of the batteries inside.

Too Many Programs Running?

Generally, new computers can run more and more programs at the same time. The kinds of programs that you run on your computer are active for a few moments at a time; they then spend the rest of their time waiting for you to type the next character or click the mouse button. They are simply waiting for something to happen. You can have several documents open at the same time.

SpyWare and Viruses are much different. They are active processes that are continually looking for a way out of your computer and access the Internet. When your computer is running, there are legitimate processes going on that need to watch your printer, keyboard, mouse and other devices. But SpyWare and Viruses have no business on your computer.

When your computer runs slower than normal, you should suspect one of these computer problems. Learn how to detect and remove them.

One technique that I use to regain control of a computer that has run wild from these problems is to activate the Task Manager by holding the CONTROL and ALT buttons and tapping the DELETE key on your keyboard. (Control - ALT - Delete). You can also activate the Task Manager by right clicking on the gray part of the Task Bar and picking Task Manager from the pop-up menu.

When viewing the processes in the Task Manager on a regular basis, you become familiar with the programs that you need to have running. You should see your anti-virus, explorer and a dozen or more programs running. You will notice some other programs running as well. Simply attempt to use the END TASK button to end some of these processes. When your computer is turned off or in "sleep mode", no programs are running. Many of these programs that you have ended are restarted when your computer is turned back on.

WHICH IS BEST FOR ME ?
INTERNET PROVIDERS
AOL
ATT
JUNO
YAHOO
SBC
COX
RR
MSN
Hudson

Which Internet Provider?

You probably know that I cannot answer that question. This depends greatly on how much you use it, and what you are looking for. Most providers are good and reliable. Be ready to switch at any time. There is no unwritten rule that you can't change your e-mail address; everyone does.

Take a little bit of time to get a secondary e-mail address. I prefer the free e-mail address from Yahoo.com. But I also have a Juno address, a Netzero address and an e-mail address from my current Internet Provider. For the bulk of my business, I use my own Domain name.

E-mail can be managed by a number of e-mail programs or through the Internet Provider's webmail feature. Learn how to use both.

High Speed Internet is fun. It also makes your software update process go much faster. Again, pick one type of service (DSL or Cable) and use it. It does not matter which one, as long as the service is fast and reliable. High Speed Internet is often called "Broadband".

You can learn about the Internet Service Providers (ISP) in your area at **www.TheList.com**.

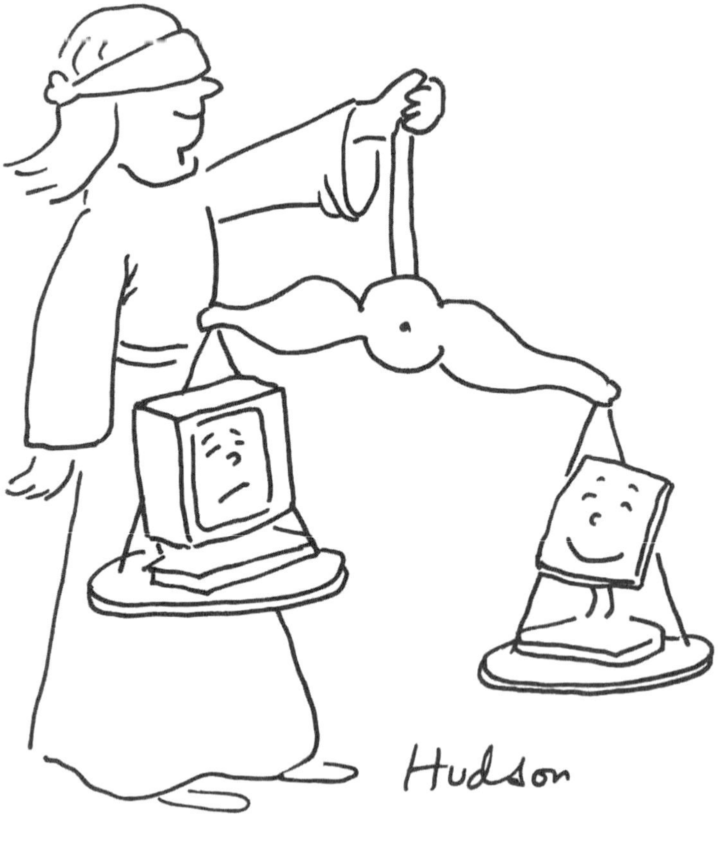

Computer Product Rating

Computer magazines are a great resource for the latest information concerning new computer products, software, security and maintenance issues. Articles and product reviews are valuable for learning what products are and how they can help you.

Much of this information is available on-line at **www.cnet.com**. You can easily find product reviews from editors and consumers. Comparisons with similar products are readily available.

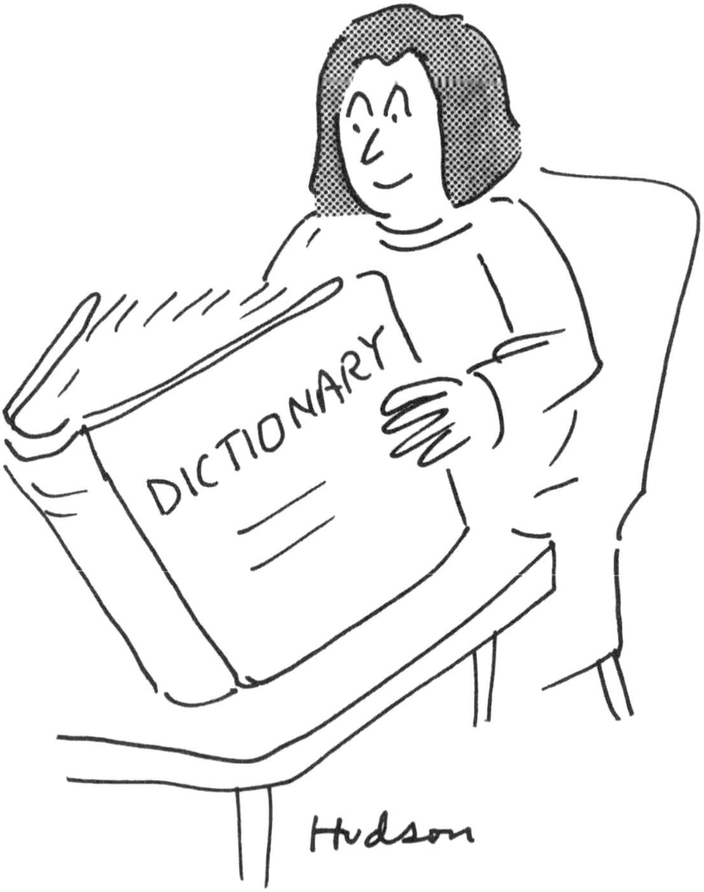
DICTIONARY
Hudson

Dictionary

Ad-aware - The brand name of LavaSoft's Anti-Spyware, Anti-Adware software, highly rated and recommended to combat this common computer problem. This program requires that you update it regularly and initiate scans.

Adware - A number of free download programs receive revenues from advertisers. These free programs may help you to save passwords, display the weather in your area, or may be a simple but colorful screensaver. These free programs show advertisements and may cause pop-up window advertisements. The best way to avoid pop-ups is to uninstall these free software programs that make your computer run slower.

Anti-Virus - Software that is designed to combat Virus software that may enter into your computer through e-mail, websites, Local Area Network connections, floppy diskettes and other media that is introduced into your computer.

Archive - Regular backups that are dated and saved, so that you can retrieve a specific version of your data.

Backup - A copy of your data in a compressed or uncompressed form which can be restored onto your computer in the event that your working copy is destroyed or corrupt. Regular backups are highly recommended since you do not know when your computer software or hardware will fail.

Blogs - Blogs is short for Web Logs. Blogs are message boards on the Internet that are developed for specific topic discussion. Generally, regular members of the Blog return to update their thoughts in the journal. Blogs are similar to eGroups, Message Boards, Guest Books and Forums.

Browser - a computer program such as Internet Explorer, Netscape and Mozilla FireFox, which allows you to visit and display websites on the Internet.

Broadband - High Speed Internet Service.

CD-Burner - A CD-ROM device that can also create CD media. Also known as CD-Writer.

CD-R - A CD-ROM media that can have your data or music copied to it through a BURN process. In most cases, your CD Burner software will use a Write All At Once method. Many CD-Burners can use a multi-session mode that will allow you to add new files to the CD at a later date. In some cases, a multi-session CD cannot be read by older CD-ROM devices. For maximum transportability, use the Write All At Once method.

CD-ROM - A plastic disk that may contain music or computer data. Many software programs are delivered on an original CD-ROM by the manufacturer.

CD-RW - A CD-ROM media that can have your data or music copied to it through a BURN process. The CD-RW media can be erased, formatted and the original data can be rewritten on it. A CD-RW may be used many times but may not be readable by other computers that have other CD drives.

Cookie - A cookie is a small file that is stored onto your computer when you are visiting a website. This file identifies you and your computer for tracking purposes. Cookies are necessary when you are making on-line purchases using an on-line shopping cart. In some cases, this practice serves no purpose. Cookies can be turned off through the Internet Options section of your Control Panel. Check the Custom level setting in the Security section.

Debug - Debug is a method of testing a program to determine the nature of its faults so that it can be corrected. You generally would not debug a program or web page if a failure occurs. If you receive an error message about a program or web page fault that asks if you

And Your Sanity Intact 81

should debug it, you would normally answer "NO". In many cases, the cause of the fault is not known to you. It could be that your computer ran out of memory space or that the program or its files became corrupt. Restarting your computer may do the trick. Saving and backing up your data is important. Reinstallation of the program may be necessary. Some programs that have been installed on your computer may interfere with your program making it non-functional. Some computer programs and updates are installed in a manner that is not reversible.

Default - This is that standard parameter setting. You can set the Default setting for most of the controls on your computer. Your Default Printer is the primary printer that you use for most things when alternate printers are available. The Default Website for Internet Explorer is www.msn.com, but you can change this setting for your Home Page to whatever website you wish.

Defrag - Defrag is a Microsoft system utility program that is designed to review the use of your disk drive and combine file fragments to use continuous disk space. This can increase the performance of your computer slightly.

Desktop - The desktop is the main display on your computer, behind any open windows, task bar, Start menu, or Icons that appear on your screen. The color or photo that appears is your desktop wallpaper. A Screensaver program changes the appearance of your display, so that the same image does not "burn" into your tube-type display monitor.

Desktop Computer - A computer that is designed to be installed at a stationary location. Desktop computers consist of a separate keyboard, mouse, video display and tower which contains the processing unit, hard disk drive, other disk drives and connectors for other devices.

Domain Name - A universal but unique name on the Internet. A domain name can be purchased and renewed annually for $35 or less. The Domain Name consists of a name and Sub-domain, such as ".com", ".org", ".net". Each Domain Name can utilize it's own sub-domains before the main name and can be used for an e-mail address. www.KeepThisComputerAlive.com is the full use of a domain name, using the sub-domain "www". The e-mail address dan@KeepThisComputerAlive.com uses the Domain Name and could be used to reach the author.

Driver - Devices that are installed on your computer become recognized and usable with the use of Driver software. Newer computers and newer devices are often "Plug and Play", so that installation becomes easier. It is important to save the original diskette or CD-ROM media that came with the devices that you added to your computer. If your computer needs to be rebuilt or replaced, you must have the software and drivers needed.

DSL - A Digital Subscriber Line provides a high speed Internet service, using a specialized DSL modem to access the DSL signal on a telephone line. This service is generally provided by the major telephone company that services the telephone lines in your community. Often, another telephone company that sells telephone service in your community resells DSL services also. The DSL service is provided through your telephone line as a non-interfering signal that allows the telephone line to be used for regular telephone service simultaneously. A DSL filter must be connected to each device that uses that telephone line, including telephones, answering machines, FAX machines and Caller ID devices. This DSL filter may fail, causing an interruption of your DSL service. If your DSL modem came with more filters than you need, do not throw the extras away, since they may be useful if the current filters fail.

DVD - DVD movies have been popularized in the entertainment industry. Many computers are equipped with DVD players and recorders, so that movies can be played on your computer. But DVD media is also used to deliver software programs and data. DVD writers and DVD-R media can hold a great deal more data than CD-ROM media, but may not be as transportable. Copying and creating your own DVD movies is technically challenging.

E-mail - Electronic mail is a form of personal communication that you can access on your computer. Many e-mail services can use e-mail programs, such as Outlook and Outlook Express; or use a webmail option where your e-mail account can be accessed through your provider's website. If your e-mail address is myname@aol.com, then you can access it from any computer by visiting www.aol.com. Many other e-mail addresses can be accessed by a similar method.

FAQ - Frequently Asked Questions is usually an electronic guide that is designed to help you with a product or service. An FAQ may be e-mailed to you, shown at a website, appear in a special file on the media that new software was delivered on or be contained within the program's HELP section.

File Types - Every file on your computer has a specific purpose and is classified as a specific file type. The File Type is identified by a three letter code that follows a period in the file name, which is known as the "file extension". The file type identifies what program or programs that the file may be used in, i.e. word processing, spreadsheet or picture. While Microsoft Windows allows known file types to be hidden, it is important to recognize file types when receiving any file that is attached to an e-mail.

Firewalls - Firewalls are a protective device or software that assists you in limiting access to your computer through a network or the Internet. Often, undesirable websites are blocked. When configured incorrectly, firewalls can severely limit or prevent Internet access.

Flash Memory - A solid state memory component that is used primarily to store data in a similar manner as a disk drive. Flash Memory is used in Digital Cameras, MP3 Players, and various Memory Sticks. These devices are very reliable but fairly expensive for long term storage as a backup device. It is great for transferring data between two computers, once the proper driver software has been installed on both.

Floppy Disk - A floppy diskette is a removable flexible media type that is used to save and transfer data and programs between computers. The current Floppy Diskette is a 3 ½ inch flexible disk that is contained inside a plastic case with a spring loaded protective door which is opened automatically when inserted into the Floppy Disk Drive. Dust and Magnets are the primary enemies of this media, which may only last 5 to 10 years.

Freeware - Software programs that are provided to you for FREE. In some cases, these programs are provided as a demo of the full version. In other cases, the software provides a vehicle of advertisement for other products. Nobody writes good software and provides it for FREE without some sort of compensation. In many cases, there is a charge for technical support on Freeware.

Hard Disk - This is the primary non-removable media type in your computer. It is most often the "C" drive, which contains the operating system and other software that is installed on your computer. Removable and External Hard Disk drives are becoming common as a secondary drive for backup and data storage. The hard disk platter is contained in a sealed metal box. It can be susceptible to damage when your computer is dropped or jarred. The hard disk unit will eventually fail, but should last for the normal life of your computer.

Hard Drive - Another term for Hard Disk.

High Speed Internet - An Internet service that is often provided through a specialized connection modem. The DSL service is provided through your telephone. High Speed Cable Internet Services are offered through your Cable Television service. High Speed Internet is often called Broadband.

HTML - Hypertext Markup Language is used to format and decorate web pages and formatted e-mail. A number of programs have been developed to make "programming" HTML easier. This includes Front Page and Dreamweaver.

Icons - Icons are a small graphic that should provide a visual clue of the program or action that it represents. To open or activate a program, you may use a method of "double click" with the left or primary button on your mouse. To select an Icon, click just once with your left or primary mouse button. A single click of the right or secondary mouse button will cause a context sensitive menu to appear, so that you can use a single left mouse click to select an alternative action. Double right click performs no function. If you have trouble using the double left click, simply use one right click to get the menu, and one left click on the option that you want. The TOP item on this menu is always the Open or Activate function that you would get if you used "double click".

Inkjet - Inkjet is a common trade name of an ink cartridge based printer. Most Inkjet cartridge based printers have one or more color cartridges and a black ink cartridge. While cartridge refilling is possible, I recommend that you review your printer's recommendation. Remember that your printer was fairly inexpensive, but the cartridges are rather expensive. I would bet that the printer manufacturer earns more money on cartridges than on the printer itself.

Internet Browser - An Internet browser is software installed on your computer which allows you to display web pages on the Internet. Internet Explorer is the most common browser. America On Line (AOL) provides custom software that includes an Internet browser window. Netscape was a very popular browser during the first few years of the Internet. Mozilla Firefox is quickly gaining popularity as an Internet browser, since it seems to be more resistant to Pop-up ads and SpyWare problems. Visit www.mozilla.org for details in downloading this free browser.

Internet Telephone - Voice Over IP technology has made regular telephone service very inexpensive. People who have a high speed Internet service can take advantage of a primary or secondary telephone service through companies like Vonage.com. These companies provide a telephone adapter that connects to the high speed Internet service. Your telephone or telephone network can then be connected to this adapter, instead of the telephone service wires that come from the street into your home.

Find a free Speed Test service on the Internet to see if your High Speed Internet can run a low cost Internet Telephone service.

IP - Internet Protocol is a method of networking used by the Internet. Each computer is assigned a unique IP Address on the Internet or local area network. A Domain Name is simply an alias to that computer's or service's IP address on the Internet or network.

ISP - Internet Service Provider is the company that sells a dial-up or high speed Internet service. This may be AOL, MSN, Earthlink or one of many other companies. A list of ISPs is maintained at www.TheList.com. One strategy to take advantage of competition between providers is to use a free e-mail address that is independent of your Internet Service Provider, such as Yahoo.com. That way you can change your service without changing your e-mail address. The other method is to buy a Domain Name that can auto-forward your e-mail to the e-mail address assigned by your current provider.

IT - Information Technology is the department or field of study of using computers to maintain and distribute data to people.

Java - Java is a programming language that is often referred to on the Internet. One confusion is that Java is also the word often used to describe JavaScript and websites.

JavaScript - A script language that can show programmable information on a website. This script language is delivered to your computer at a webpage or in e-mail so that it is executed by your computer. This is operated on a temporary basis, but uses memory that can slow down your other computer operations. A web page may fail to load completely when all memory resources have been used.

Laptop Computer - A small, lightweight and portable computer. When necessary, laptops can provide great portability. But these computers are often delicate and more expensive than desktop computers. Add-ons are often more expensive, since they use proprietary parts. Backup is even more important since these computers may not last as long as desktop computers. If your Laptop Computer provides fold-out feet underneath, this is often a necessary component of the computer's cooling system. Use the Feet or lose the computer from overheat.

Laser Printer - A laser printer uses toner like a photo copying machine and "burns" your printed image onto the paper. Laser printers produce quality, non-streaking printouts at a lower cost than ink based printers. Low cost laser printers can suffer from overheat. In many cases, printing runs on personal laser printers should be limited to 10 or 20 sheets at a time, to allow cooling. Overheating may damage the toner cartridge or paper feed mechanism. Color Laser Printers run even hotter and should be treated accordingly. For high volume printing, estimate your volume and research to find the laser printer that meets your needs. If the laser printer does not provide the volume specification, then don't buy it. In many cases, the repair of low cost laser printers is as high as buying a new printer.

Local Area Network (LAN) - Through the use of a Router, computers within the same area can be networked together to share an Internet connection, printers and data with each other. The Local Area Network is fairly inexpensive and easy to maintain. It also can add additional safety from the Internet as a result of using the router. A Local Area Network may be established using Ethernet cables or through wireless network adapters.

Maximize - A button near the top right corner of a window will cause the window to be redrawn to take up most of the screen. Clicking on this button again will restore the window to the original size and position. Sometimes a window is displayed OFF the normal window. Accessing the MAXIMIZE button can force the window to be displayed fully in the viewable part of the normal screen. Each program window is also represented by an Icon that appears on your Task bar at the bottom of the screen. You can maximize a window by using your right or secondary mouse button to display a menu. Then use the left or primary mouse button to select MAXIMIZE.

Memory - Memory usually refers to the usable Random Access Memory (RAM) that is installed inside your computer. This is a fast electronic device that is used by programs that are currently running. Virtual memory is an area of your hard disk drive that can temporarily store information by programs and datasets that do not fit entirely in the existing RAM memory. The use of Virtual memory does allow the program(s) to continue running, but at a much slower rate.

Menu Bar - The menu bar appears on each window immediately below the Title Bar. The menu is oriented with words, where submenus appear below each word in a pull down fashion.

Minimize - A button near the top right corner of a window will cause the window to disappear from the screen. To restore this window to the original size and position, click on that window's Icon which appears on your Task bar at the bottom of the screen.

Modem - A modem is a specialized service connection device for telephone dial-up, DSL Internet Service or Cable High Speed Internet Service. Most telephone dial-up services now use a 56K modem. DSL and Cable Internet services usually provide the specific modem that is compatible with their service. The specification of your service should be determined if you want or need to replace your modem. In many cases, your cable Internet provider must be contacted to activate your service for using the new modem. Lightning and other voltage conditions can damage your modem. It is often impossible to completely isolate your modem from these transient conditions. Sometimes dial-up modems fail to connect, or fail to disconnect.

Mouse - The mouse is the most popular pointing device for your computer. I recommend the use of an optical mouse, since it contains fewer moving parts. A Wireless mouse can be nice, but most also carry batteries, so they become heavier and harder to move. The roller ball of a standard mouse can get dirty as can the rollers inside the mouse. The wire that connects your mouse to your computer can easily be broken, causing the mouse to run wild.

Notebook Computer - see Laptop computer. Notebook Computer is a more appropriate name, since these computers are often hard to use when positioned in your lap. Good posture helps to prevent a number of muscular, joint and nerve damage problems.

Operating System - Your computer comes equipped with a low level operating system that you see for a moment when you first turn your computer on. (Often referred to as BIOS). The Windows system is a high level operating system that is installed on your hard drive; you use it to control your programs, devices and data.

P2P Sharing - Peer to Peer Sharing is a capability where two computers on the Internet can share files. Programs such as Napster, Kazaa and Warez are used by their subscribers to locate others to share files, such as music.

Parallel Printer - Older printers came with a thicker parallel printer cable. At the printer, the cable has a two row, 36 pin connector. At the computer end is a two row, D shaped connector with 25 pins. Many newer computers do not have the parallel printer port, but a USB to Parallel Printer adapter is available.

Phishing - This is a form of on-line Identity Theft, where a SPOOF e-mail is sent, as if it comes to the user from a bank, PayPal, eBay or other institution. The e-mail contains a form, where the user is duped into logging in with their account name and password. These organizations would absolutely NEVER use e-mail to contact you about verifying your password. For more information about Scams, Fraud and Identity Theft, read *Don't Get Ripped Off! Get Help! Tell it to George*, by Cynthia Bercowetz.

POP Server - Your e-mail can be read from a so-called Post Office Protocol Server (POP) address. Your e-mail address contains a Domain Name section, such as "Earthlink.com". If you do not know the proper address for getting your e-mail, you can often find this by checking their website at the same Domain Name. In some cases, you are receiving e-mail from one Domain but using your Internet service provider to send e-mail. Your SMPT Server address may be different for sending e-mail.

Power Conditioners - A power conditioner is an electrical device that provides clean electrical power for computers and electronic devices. This can reduce computer outage from power surges and brown-out conditions. While this product can reduce about 90% of the outages, it can't produce temporary electrical supply like a UPS can when the power is off. The advantage of the power conditioner is that its long term cost is much lower, since a battery does not need to be replaced. Notebook computers already have battery and power conditioning built-in.

Program - A computer program is "software" that can be installed and registered to operate on your computer to fulfill a specific need. It often requires the original installation disk and key code for registration and licensing. Be sure to maintain the disk and key code that came with the program, so that you can reinstall it if you must restore your existing computer or if you buy a new one. Review the license agreement before installing it on additional computers.

Quick Launch Tray - The Quick Launch Tray is a row of Icons that may appear on your task bar. Program shortcuts that appear on the Quick Launch Tray can be operated by a single click on that program's Quick Launch Tray's Icon.

RAM (Random Access Memory) - Random Access Memory or RAM, refers to the solid state memory devices that are installed inside your computer that are used by programs that are currently operating on your computer. If your computer is equipped with 256MB RAM, you may be able to add more of these components to your computer. There are many different brands and specifications that may or may not work in your computer.

Restore - Several methods to Restore your computer are possible. Windows XP and Windows ME provide a Restore Point method to restore the computer's registry to the settings of a previous date. Your computer may have been shipped to you with a set of Restore disks that will allow you to perform a partial or full Restore to "like new" condition. The most drastic restoration of the full Restore would re-initialize your hard drive and install the programs that

And Your Sanity Intact 91

came with your computer. Good backups should be verified before using the Restore feature. It might be best to create additional backups before using Restore.

Router - A Router provides a local area network capability and usually includes a firewall to your Internet connection that can be shared with all of the computers on your network. While a wireless router is available, the first computer should be wired directly to the router for accessing setup and status.

Safe Mode - The Windows operating system can be restarted in Safe Mode by tapping the F8 key during startup, and by selecting the startup mode from a menu that appears. Safe Mode initiates your computer with many services and functions disabled, so your computer can be diagnosed. Scandisk and Defrag programs work faster from Safe Mode.

Scandisk - This is a handy system utility that is found in the Start menu's Program files under Accessories and System Tools. You can use this to test your hard drive or floppy diskettes to see if they are reliable. Bad sectors are marked as bad, so the disk can be used. Stray and bad files are marked and stored into files that you will probably just delete. Windows usually performs a scandisk automatically when the computer has been turned off without using the Shut Down feature from the Start menu.

Screensaver - A program or feature of Windows that displays moving graphics or blanks out your screen, so that an image is not "burned" into television type video display monitors. Windows comes with the screensaver program that you need. Third party screensavers often deliver pop-up ads. I recommend that you use the screensaver that came with Windows, and don't use a separate or third party program. Right click on the desktop and pick Properties from the menu. Then click on Screensaver and pick the screensaver that you want. You can program the delay time.

Script - A script is often a set of program control steps that adds display elements to a website or program. While most scripts perform the designed function, some scripts or "macros" for

Microsoft Word and other products may contain viruses and cause other destructive or unnecessary actions.

Search Engine - The Internet contains a large number of search engines that can help you locate information about any topic. I prefer using **google.com**.

Serial Port - This is a 9 pin D shaped connector on many computers. This was a standard port for devices that were connected to computers. Most newer devices use USB ports instead. But many older Digital Cameras, GPS devices, external modems and even some printers are connected to a serial port.

SMTP Server - Your Internet service provider (ISP) provides you with a Post Office Protocol based Internet address for sending e-mail from your e-mail program. When your e-mail does not work, you can always log into the webmail option of your e-mail to send from that. You might also get a free e-mail address from Yahoo or other provider, so you can send e-mail to people when problems occur, since these website based e-mail programs do not require your ISP provided SMTP server.

Software - Software is usually referred to as Programs.

SPAM - Unsolicited e-mail that you do not want is referred to as SPAM. In general, unscrupulous marketers that buy and maintain extensive e-mail address lists initiate SPAM. Most Internet Providers do not allow their customers to send out unsolicited e-mail in this fashion. So-called "Spammers" have the ability to send out thousands of e-mails per hour. Finding just one customer that wishes to buy or donate to their cause will only justify their method. Absolutely NEVER buy anything that is offered in a SPAM message. Don't help to make this form of advertising profitable. Never respond to a SPAM message.

Spoof - The dictionary says "Nonsense; tomfoolery; hoax; satirical imitation or a light parody". SpyWare, SPAM and Viruses use your e-mail address to send out messages in your name or someone else's from your address book with the intent to fool others into opening damaging or fraudulent e-mail. The Federal Trade Commission says that this is already illegal. In most cases, a SPOOF e-mail is an attempt to use the Internet for fraud or Identity Theft purposes. See Phishing.

SpyBot - SpyBot Search and Destroy is a popular Anti-SpyWare software program that can protect and clean your computer from this problem. It does require that you check to see if it has been updated, and you should manually initiate a scan on a regular basis.

SpyWare - Websites and e-mail can often install unwanted software onto your computer without your knowledge or permission. SpyWare can cause Pop-up ads, track your Internet access and browsing habits, record your keystrokes and report this to their tracking services. This is an invasion of your privacy. This is an unfair way to advertise their products to you. While SpyWare may be designed to do no harm to your computer, having dozens of SpyWare programs running on your computer slows or stops your computer from functioning properly. The Federal Trade Commission says that this is already illegal. Absolutely NEVER buy anything that is offered in a pop-up ad. Don't help to make this form of advertising profitable.

Start Button - The Start Button appears on the lower left corner of your computer screen on the Task Bar. Click once with your left or primary mouse button to display the Start Menu.

Start Menu - The Start Menu is displayed when you click on the Start Button. Computer program shortcuts are organized in the Start menu. Controls for your Devices, Internet Connection and other settings are listed in the Control Panel of the Settings section. A Find or Search function can help you find files on your computer. A Help Section can provide some guidance on how to do things on your computer. But this Help Section only contains information about the Windows Operating System itself and not the programs themselves.

Status Bar - The Status Bar appears at the bottom of most windows. In many cases, it displays information about the file or data that you are working with a specific program.

Surge Protector - A Surge Protector can help to protect your computer from small voltage variations. A surge protector may not prevent lightning and high energy voltage transients from doing harm to your computer. Your computer should be turned off and the power switch of the Surge Protector should be turned off to provide the best protection when lightning threatens.

Task Bar - The task bar runs along the bottom of the screen. The Start Button appears on the left side; the clock appears on the right side. Quick Launch Icons may be displayed. A slightly larger Icon will appear on the task bar for each program that is running. When a program is Minimized, you may click on that program's Icon to restore its window to the last size and position on the screen.

TCP/IP - TCP/IP is a communication protocol for local area networks and the Internet. See IP.

Title Bar - The title bar appears at the top of each window. A small Icon that identifies the window's program appears on the left side. Text appears on the title bar, which may include the name of the currently opened document and the name of the program that is running. At the far right, the Close button, Maximize and Minimize buttons appear. When Maximized, the Maximize button becomes the Restore Down button.

Toolbars - Toolbars are an optional row of action buttons that appear on a window. This usually appears immediately below the Menu Bar. Toolbars may be added or removed from the window through the View menu item. Each toolbar is named in the Toolbar selection menu with a checkbox that appears when the toolbar is selected for display.

Tower - Most Desktop computers are built into a mini tower configuration. These are designed to stand up on the floor. The CD Drive, Floppy Disk Drive and USB ports are easily accessible from the front. The Central Processing Unit, memory, hard disk drive and other components are located inside the tower. For the most part, these components come from many possible manufacturers. These are standard components and the prices of these components are minimized through the fierce competition.

Uninterruptible Power Supply (UPS) - One option for your computer is the Uninterruptible Power Supply. This device provides several minutes of electrical power when the main power source is interrupted. While the batteries are replaceable in many units, the entire unit cost is often about the same price. When power is lost, the whole idea is to SAVE the data that you were working on, and turn off your computer before the batteries go dead. The power may be restored within a few minutes, so there is no rush to turn off your computer. Test your UPS regularly.

URL - Uniform Resource Locator, which is used to specify what resource you want to reach on the Internet. The website address or Domain Name is a part of the full address, following the resource protocol "http://". When using a typical Internet browser, you often do not need to type the resource protocol of the address.

USB - The Universal Serial Bus is very popular with newer computers. New devices can be plugged into the USB port while the computer is turned on. Many devices are automatically installed and configured by the Windows system when these devices are plugged in for the first time. A disk accompanies the device, which should be stored in a safe place for later reinstallation.

Virus - Any program that is intentionally or unintentionally installed on your computer that uses any technique to spread to other computers. Virus programs may be designed to do harm to your computer, but may only attempt to cause pop-up advertisements or send out e-mail. Some viruses will restart your computer in an attempt to reconfigure your computer in hopes to improve its connection to networks or the Internet.

Wallpaper - The wallpaper is the background color or graphic of your desktop. This is set by right clicking the desktop and selecting

Properties. The color and file setting appears on the Background section.

Web Hosting Service - Websites reside on computers on the Internet through a Web hosting service. A web hosting service may provide just a simple webpage or dozens of services, such as guestbook, blogs, shopping cart, form mail and on-line database services. My favorite provider is **www.see-ct.com**.

Window - Most programs display information through a window. This window usually has standardized controls that make it easy to become familiar with any software that is installed on your computer. Title Bar, Menu Bar, Toolbars and Status Bars are typical of some of these controls.

Worm - A worm is a specific type of virus, which is designed to travel quickly through computers on the Internet. They are often simpler and smaller, inflicting less damage, so each afflicted computer can help to propagate this virus even more.

Zip Disk - A Zip Disk is a proprietary removable drive, manufactured by Iomega. Zip Disk technology is faster and holds a great deal more information than a conventional floppy disk. For the most part, writeable CD-ROMs, like CD-RW disks and CD-RW drives hold even more data and are more reliable over the years.

Zip File - A Zip File is a compressed file or folder that is used to easily transmit through the Internet. Windows XP contains the compression/decompression technique in its Windows Explorer program.

Additional Resources for Computer Terms
www.webopedia.com
www.techdictionary.com
www.computerdictionary.info

Keep Your Computer Alive CHECKLIST

- Disk Cleanup — Daily or Weekly
- Backup — Daily or Weekly
- Scandisk — Weekly
- Defrag — Monthly
- Ad-aware Updates & Scan — Daily or Weekly
- SpyBot Updates & Scan — Daily or Weekly
- Anti-Virus Updates & Scan — Weekly
- Windows Updates, — Monthly
  look for Critical & Security Updates
- Test UPS batteries — Monthly
  (uninterruptible power supply)
- Uninstall Unused Programs — Monthly
  look for unused programs
- Stop File Sharing — Daily
  look for File Sharing and disable it
- Vacuum Dust — Weekly
  from desktop, tower & monitor case

Websites in this Book

Coast Memory	CoastMemory.com
Family Internet Safety	kids.getnetwise.org
SpyBot Search & Destroy	spybot.safer-networking.de/en
c|net	www.cnet.com
Ad-aware	www.lavasoftusa.com
Mozilla FireFox	www.mozilla.org
Norton Ghost	www.symantec.com/ghost
Norton GoBack	www.symantec.com/goback
Norton Antivirus	www.symantec.com/nav/nav_pro
Internet Service Providers	www.TheList.com
Computer term dictionaries	www.computerdictionary.info www.techdictionary.com www.webopedia.com
ZoneAlarm	www.zonelabs.com

Future Computers

Nobody can predict what the future computer will look like. Flat Panel Monitors, wireless mouse and keyboards are great. The industry is considering the Set-top Box again, where your programs and data would be stored on a managed computer located somewhere on the Internet. At your home or office, you would have an Internet device that has a great screen, keyboard, mouse, speaker, microphone and a tiny device that connects it all. There will be no maintenance issues to the user in the ideal sense. Software, disk space, printing services, backup and archival services will all be rented. It is not a matter of "if I break my computer," because you simply "can't".

WebTV will be considered the grandfather of this new system.

The amount of money and time that people spend on managing their computer is often unbelievable. Many will spend hours talking to technical support specialists, only to learn that they called the wrong vendor. The Microsoft technician was simply the wrong person to talk to about a sound problem. The Dell technician was the wrong person to talk to about a printer problem. Is it hardware, or is it software?

Until the future arrives, we must explore and learn about the new innovations that enhance and protect our computer.

Index

Ad-aware, 23, 52, 79, 97
Adware, 79
Anti-Virus, 19, 33, 58, 79, 97
Archive, 79
Backup, 1, 6, 42, 45, 79, 86, 97
Blogs, 79
Broadband, 75, 80, 84
CD-Burner, 42, 80
CD-R, 45, 50, 80, 82, 96
CD-ROM, 45, 80, 82, 96
CD-RW, 45, 80, 96
Cookie, 80
Debug, 80
Default, 81
Defrag, 6, 54, 55, 81, 91, 97
Desktop, 10, 81, 94
Desktop computer, 81, 94
Domain Name, 36, 81, 86, 89, 95
Driver, 82
DSL, 27, 75, 82, 84, 88
DVD, 45, 82
E-mail, 82
FAQ, 83
File Types, 30, 83
Firewalls, 27, 83
Flash Memory, 45, 83
Floppy Disk, 83, 94
Freeware, 84
Hard Disk, 84
Hard Drive, 84
High Speed Internet, 75, 84, 88
HTML, 84

Icons, 9, 10, 81, 84, 90, 94
Inkjet, 68, 85
Internet Browser, 85
Internet Telephone, 85
IP, 85, 86, 94
ISP, 75, 86, 92
IT, 2, 86
Java, 86
JavaScript, 86
Laptop Computer, 86
Laser Printer, 87
Local Area Network, 79, 87
Maximize, 10, 87, 94
Memory, 62, 83, 87, 90
Menu Bar, 88, 94, 96
Minimize, 10, 88, 94
Modem, 88
Mouse, 65, 71, 88
Notebook Computer, 88
Operating System, 62, 89, 93
P2P, 29, 89
Parallel Printer, 89
Phishing, 89, 93
POP Server, 89
Power Conditioners, 17, 90
Program, 5, 10, 42, 90, 91
Quick Launch Tray, 10, 90
RAM, 87, 90
Restore, 10, 42, 43, 50, 90, 94
Router, 27, 87, 91
Safe Mode, 54, 91
Scandisk, 6, 54, 55, 91, 97
Screensaver, 81, 91
Script, 30, 91
Search Engine, 92

Serial Port, 92
SMTP Server, 92
Software, 6, 42, 58, 60, 79, 84, 92, 101
SPAM, 35, 36, 92
Spoof, 92
SpyBot, 23, 24, 93, 97
SpyWare, 1, 6, 23, 33, 39, 42, 52, 58, 60, 73, 85, 92, 93
Start Button, 10, 93, 94
Start Menu, 93
Status Bar, 12, 94, 96
Surge Protector, 1, 17, 94
Task Bar, 10, 64, 73, 93, 94
TCP/IP, 94
Title Bar, 10, 88, 94, 96

Toolbars, 10, 94, 96
Tower, 94
Uninstall, 6, 57, 79, 97
UPS, 17, 95, 97
URL, 95
USB, 45, 65, 66, 89, 92, 94, 95
Virus, 19, 79, 95
Wallpaper, 10, 95
Web hosting service, 96
WebTV, 101
Window, 10, 96
Worm, 96
Zip Disk, 96
Zip File, 96

I.
RULES
BACKUP
SCAN
DEFRAG
II.
ANTI
SPYWARE
VIRUS
SPAM
Hudson

Paradigms - Computer Longevity

This section lists specific tips that are scattered throughout this book. This collection of statements forms a guideline to keeping your computer running in top shape.

Anti-virus and anti-SpyWare updates are ... necessary ... against the newest threats. 60
Any computer that is on the Internet and does not have anti-virus software has a virus. 19
Backward compatibility to the older media types is not guaranteed 45
Color laser printers are even more susceptible to damage by overheating 69
Computer maintenance functions are vital to good computer health 15
Data is not guaranteed ... on ... older magnetic media...................45
Do not open unknown or uncharacteristic e-mail messages 39
E-mail can be managed by ... e-mail programs or ... webmail ... Learn ... both 75
Every person ... must work a little extra to keep their computer working 2
Get a secondary e-mail address ... from Yahoo.com.....................75
If it ain't broke, don't fix it..60
If you do not backup your data someday you will lose it................43
Laser printers run quite hot... and ...are not designed to run continuously 68
Maintain a free web-based e-mail address ... for registering products 35
People ... know instinctively that computers might crash at any minute 47
Safe Mode is an important troubleshooting feature of Windows....54
Some people have trouble with a wireless optical mouse ... they are heavier ... because of the weight of the batteries inside. 71
Someday your computer will die..2

Surge Protectors do not provide protection against severe lightning 17
When you have to restore the computer, software must be reinstalled 42
When your computer runs slower than normal, you should suspect SpyWare or Viruses 73
Windows 95 ... that computer is ... ready for the scrap heap........... 1
Write down all ... passwords, ... registration numbers ... so you can access these accounts 52
You never know when the set of backup disks that you use will suddenly stop working, leaving you without a backup 43
You should have the Restore and Software Disks of every program that you have purchased and installed. 42
You should only have ONE Anti-virus software program installed 20
Your computer gets worse, faster, when you share it with children. 33

visit www.KeepYourComputerAlive.com